CD INCLUDED

THE BEGINNER'S GUIDE TO
ELECTRONIC DRUMS

An Introduction to Electronic Drums and Percussion

by Bob Terry

Edited by Donny Gruendler

All music performed and programmed by
Bob Terry

All audio recorded, mixed, and mastered by
Donny Gruendler at Inc. Studios

Illustrations by
Donny Gruendler and Jon Hastings

This book is dedicated to the memory of
Jane Terry

ISBN 978-1-61780-427-4

HAL•LEONARD®
CORPORATION
7777 W. BLUEMOUND RD. P.O. BOX 13819 MILWAUKEE, WI 53213

In Australia Contact:
Hal Leonard Australia Pty. Ltd.
4 Lentara Court
Cheltenham, Victoria, 3192 Australia
Email: ausadmin@halleonard.com.au

Copyright © 2011 by HAL LEONARD CORPORATION
International Copyright Secured   All Rights Reserved

No part of this publication may be reproduced in any form or by any means
without the prior written permission of the Publisher.

Visit Hal Leonard Online at
www.halleonard.com

TABLE OF CONTENTS

TRACK LISTING

PREFACE

On one hand it's rather ironic that I have authored a book entitled *The Beginners Guide to Electronic Drums* as I have never really thought of myself as an electronic drummer. On the other hand, who better to write the book? Especially when you consider that I have utilized this technology within my performances and daily work routine for the past twenty-five years.

Drummers

As drummers, we don't want to admit that we are caveman-like and bang on wooden things. Each of us would like to think that there is a bit more to the art form. Yet, I have had many conversations with drummers and seen comments on the drum forums such as, "Electronic drums will never replace real drums" and, "People who play electronic drums don't know how to play real drums." Most don't even say, "Acoustic drums," they say "real" drums. Well, at one time real drums were hollowed logs. I think this distaste comes from the fear of the unknown, the unfamiliar. For example: Did electric guitars replace acoustic guitars? Did electronic pianos replace acoustic pianos? Did the synthesizer replace the violin, oboe, or flute? The answers to all of these questions are unquestionably *No*. So why should drummers believe that the electronic kit will replace their trusty acoustic kit?

Bumps in the Road for This Real Drummer

Like other acoustic drummers, I was slow to implement electronic drums into my workflow. The first electronic drum that I saw (and played) was in a recording studio during the 1970s. It wasn't actually a whole kit, but it had a module and three or four plastic molded toms with foam rubber under a plastic head. I was doing this jingle (for a commercial) and they made "dew-dew-dew-dew" sounds. It sounded awful! The jingle should have been a cartoon, but I'm sorry to say that it wasn't at all.

During the 1980s, I began to hear hand claps and white noise on snare drum backbeats and automated percussion on most radio songs. It was very apparent that technology had entered the drum world. In 1985, I got a call to play with Wang Chung, a British pop band from London. Wang Chung was known for its digitally sampled drum sounds, and for being one of the first bands to use digital equipment. I had no experience with any of this technology at the time, but it was here to stay. Over the next few years, I learned about triggering, MIDI, and digital audio. Thank goodness I was paying attention…

Present Day Move to Explanation

I now work with the Yamaha Corporation of America and act as a consultant for their DTX electronic drum brand. I work alongside many of today's top drummers and help them with their electronic drumming needs. In addition, I have also grown comfortable incorporating twenty first century electronics into my own drumming, both in the recording studio and during live performances.

Scope

No matter if you are a beginner or a world touring pro, this text will explore electronic drums in great detail. I will present the types of gear, various manufacturers, user-case scenarios, terminology, and all the "extras" you will need to use this technology.

I hope you enjoy the book. It's an honor to be able to share my knowledge and learning experiences with you.

ACKNOWLEDGMENTS

Editor
I first must thank my editor and good friend, Donny Gruendler. This book would not have been possible without Donny's expertise, support, commitment, and patience. I will be forever grateful. To learn more about Donny, please visit: www. donnygruendler.com.

Family
Thanks to my wife, Julie, for her love, support, and being my best friend. I don't know of anyone who would have put up with my constant "tapping" for so many years; Ethan and Madison Terry for their understanding of Daddy's drumming affliction; Robert Anderson Terry Sr. for his guidance, wisdom, and support: "Son, keep it simple, solid, and steady and you will do fine;" Susi Tobin, my sister, for her love and support and for being my biggest fan.

Friends and Colleagues
Thanks to Shaun Tomson, World Champion surfer, author, entrepreneur, and motivational speaker for giving me the courage and confidence to write this book. Thanks to my friends at Yamaha Corporation of America (and Japan) for their support. I would especially like to thank Athan Billias, Director of Marketing, for his guidance and confidence; Tom Griffin, DTX Drums Product Marketing Specialist, for his support and for sharing his expertise; John Wittmann, Nicole Proctor, and Jennifer Vierling (from Yamaha Artist Relations) for allowing me to be part of the team; Jun Aoki, Satoshi Kido, and Makoto Katsuura at Yamaha Corporation of Japan for their expertise and support of DTX Electronic Drums; Yamaha Acoustic drum team: David Jewell, Jim Haler, Greg Crane, Prudence Elliott, and Daryl Anderson for their support; YCA management for their support: Rick Young, Tom Sumner, Garth Gilman, and Yoichi Oba; Alan McPherson and Brian McGovern at Steinberg North America for their support, help, and guidance; John Emrich for his expertise (and advice); Derek Zimmerman, John Roderick, and Julia Truchsess at Gen16 for their support. To the Guitar Center Drum Department: Mark Nelson, Jeff Lorenz, and Glenn Noyes; Musician's Friend's Randy Pratt; and Sam Ash Hollywood Drum manager, John Parker—thank you all for your invaluable insight on the electronic drum industry; Tim Pederson at Musician's Institute for his support and partnership. Thanks to Julian Colbeck and Terry Shields at KeyFax New Media for their expertise and support; David Levine at Full Circle Management for his insights on the drum and percussion market and industry; Steve Fisher at Roland Corporation for his support and contribution. Last (but certainly not least), to all of my Brothers in Arms and talented pro drummer friends that I work with and who have contributed to the book: a big, big, big THANK YOU!

A special thank you to the following:
Abel Vallejo, Adam Topol, Alan and Gigi White, Billy Ward, Carlos Guzman, Chad Wright, Chaun Horton, Chris Bailey, Chris Hesse, Cole and Cheryl Marcus, Donnell Spencer Jr., Felix "Da Kat" Pollard, Gorden Campbell, John Blackwell, John Mahon, Kenny Aronoff, Matt Sorum, Mark Bennett, Mark Zonder, Marvin McQuitty Jr., Mike Bordin, Mike Johnston, Ndugu Chancler, Paul Leim, Ralph Humphrey, Ray Luzier, Reek Havok, Richie Bravo, Russ Miller, Shauney Baby, Teddy Campell, Tony Escapa, Tony Verderosa, and Zak Bond.

Companies
Thanks to all of the companies that have supported me through the years: Yamaha Corporation of America, DW Drums Inc., Zildjian Inc., Vater Inc., XL Specialty Percussion Inc., Shure Brothers, Inc., Steinberg North America, Inc., FXpansion Inc., Notion Music Inc., Fat Congas Inc., ButtKicker Inc., and KickPort Inc.

ABOUT THE AUTHOR

Bob Terry, originally from Indianapolis, Indiana, started playing the drums at age three. It's a common story for drummer types: he banged on pots and pans until he got a set of drums. In his late teens, Bob attended Indiana University and majored in music performance. Terry soon moved to Los Angeles and quickly formed a relationship with A&R guru, Jon Koladner and Geffen Records. He worked with many of the artists on the label throughout the eighties and, in 1985, Bob started working with Wang Chung. Together, they appeared in the William Friedkin directed movie (and corresponding music video) *To Live and Die in L.A.* Tours, radio, television, and personal appearances soon followed. These early experiences have helped to spawn a thirty-five-plus year career in the music industry.

In the nineties, Bob took some time off from touring. He moved to Santa Barbara, California and started a family. During this period he began working in sales and marketing for various music instrument manufacturers. Before long, Bob was playing drums behind many of the artists that appeared at the NAMM (National Association of Music Merchants) show. Currently, Terry is playing live, doing session work, and working as a consultant for Yamaha's DTX electronic drum division. Bob also manages the DTX artist relations and works with some of the best drummers in the world on electronic percussion. To learn more about Bob, visit: www.bobterrydrums.com.

INTRODUCTION

Electronic drums have been available since the 1970s. What was once a very crude instrument has now evolved into a very sophisticated, easy-to-use tool. This is true for both the beginner and seasoned professional. I have never believed that electronic drums should replace acoustic drums. However, there are many musical situations where electronic drums should be used, whether exclusively or in a hybrid type of situation alongside an acoustic drumset.

Reality

Just about everything we hear in today's popular music has electronic drums, sounds, or loops present within it. Obviously, in most cases the drummer is playing the drums, but he could also be playing alongside a preset pattern (loop) or triggering a sampled sound. In the recording studio, producers usually craft unique sounds on both the snare and kick drum. Additionally, it's now typical for a major recording artist to require their touring drummer to sound exactly like that studio recording, i.e., unique snare and kick drum sound (while playing live). To do this, the drummer is required to trigger the "studio samples" of each drum sound from their drum module, percussion pad, or hybrid setup.

Assumptions

It is important to realize that this book is a *beginners guide* to electronic drumming. Therefore, this text is intended to *introduce* the fundamental concepts contained within electronic drums and percussion. This is accomplished through detailed explanations of each type of device, its professional uses (and common scenarios), the popular manufacturers, and the main features and benefits of utilizing electronics. As with all technology-based products, the learning curve is infinite and it is constantly changing. Thus, if you need any additional information on electronic drums, sampling, MIDI, and software, there are many fine books and online resources available.

Illustrations, Notation, and Audio

For illustration purposes and the sake of clarity, I have chosen to use Yamaha DTX products exclusively. However, many manufacturers' products can be utilized. Furthermore, I have also notated many of the grooves that I perform on the CD. Thus, it is assumed that you can read basic drum notation. If you cannot, I highly suggest that you find a reputable teacher in your area.

CHAPTER ONE
Full Electronic Drum Kit

Prominent Electronic Drum Manufacturers	Predominant Models
Yamaha	DTX900 Series, DTX700 Series, DTX500 Series
Roland	TD V-Pro Series, V-Stage Series, V-Tour Series
Alesis	DM 10 Pro, DM6 USB Express, USB Pro
Pearl	ePro Live
Simmons	SD5K, SD7PK, SD9PK
2Box	DrumIt Five

A full electronic drum kit is the synthetic counterpart to the traditional acoustic drumset. It contains pads that correspond to each acoustic voice, such as the bass drum, snare drum, toms, hi-hat, and cymbals. There is also a module that acts as the central nervous system of the setup. As such, each pad connects to this module, which then reproduces the various tones, timbres, and drum sounds that have been sampled (or modeled) from an acoustic drumset. Altogether, this drum kit performs in a very similar manner to your current drumset.

In this chapter, we will discuss the advantages of using (and the many professional uses for) the full electronic drum kit. In addition, a detailed description of each kit component, how to hook up these components, audio samples, and a quick look at my onstage setup will also be presented.

Fig. 1.1. Examples of Electronic Drum Kits

ELECTRONIC ADVANTAGES

There are many advantages to using a full electronic drum kit. These include controlling volume and having multiple drum sound and instrument options, as well as the ability to produce high-quality recorded drum sounds (regardless of your studio environment). In addition, there are many practice tools included within today's modules, such as an on-board metronome and software features that can analyze the timing of your grooves, fills, and overall beat placement. Let's take a look at each advantage in greater detail:

VOLUME

The most obvious (and popular) advantage of the electronic kit is the ability to control the output performance volume. Although drummers should learn to play at all volume levels, the acoustic drumset is still a relatively loud instrument. Therefore, the ability to play with headphones or "turn down" an amplifier is a serious plus for practicing drummers who live in apartments. It is even more critical for performance-minded drummers who regularly play in sensitive volume venues like churches, houses of worship, casinos, and upscale restaurants. Furthermore, many high profile touring drummers work for leaders who prefer in-ear monitors and a low stage volume. Again, the full electronic kit works perfectly well in this situation.

PRACTICE TOOLS

Many electronic drum kits are packaged with an on-board metronome, or click track, that can help you to practice and play in time. Not only can you set this to a specific tempo (BPM/beats per minute). but you can also assign it to a wood block, cowbell, or shaker sound too. Most models also contain a type of "Groove Check" or "Rhythm Coach" that is able to analyze how steady you are playing alongside a metronome or sequenced song. Some advanced modules also feature a sophisticated "Rhythm Gate," which cancels out (stops the playback) of any stroke that you play out of time. Altogether, these practice tools function as an on-board drum instructor, which can help you progress in a systematic (and analytical) manner.

INSTRUMENT OPTIONS

Electronic drums also have the ability to produce many different drum kit sounds. For example, many modules allow you to choose any shell type used in acoustic drum manufacturing such as oak, maple, beech, and birch. Additionally, these kits also utilize various presets tuned for each music style. These usually include rock, pop, metal, jazz, 1970s studio, 1980s arena, and beyond. Other presets focus on world percussion instruments such as congas, bongos, timbales, triangles, wood blocks, and maracas. Specialized, and oftentimes expensive, modules also offer various chromatically tuned timpanis, marimbas, xylophones, and vibraphones. You can also add "on-board" effects such as compression, reverb, and flange to each of your drum sounds, preset kits, and percussion instruments. As if this was not enough, today's modules allow you to tweak each sound, remap any sound to any pad, and save them as your own custom kits.

RECORDING: IN THE MODULE

Many kits allow you to record your drumming performance within (and on) the module itself. This is a great feature for creating loops or patterns. You can play these back on stage during performances or use them as entertaining practice tools.

RECORDING: STUDIO REPLACEMENT

Most of us do not own (or have regular access to) an expensive and finely tuned recording studio. With today's technology, you do not need one! With today's crop of electronic drum kits, you can make a high-quality drumset recording in your bedroom, garage, living room, or basement. All you will need is your electronic set, a computer, and DAW recording software such as Cubase, Pro Tools, Logic, or Ableton Live. Many pro drummers have set up this kind of home studio. They record their electronic kit into the computer and upload their recordings via the Internet—to their clients, who might be anywhere in the world.

COMPONENTS

Just like acoustic drumsets, an electronic drum kit is comprised of many individual components. These include pads that correspond to each acoustic drum voice: the bass drum, snare drum, toms, hi-hat, and cymbals. There is also a module that acts as the central nervous system of the setup. As such, each pad connects to this module by cable. Then, when a pad is struck, the module reproduces the appropriate on-board drum or percussion sound.

Each electronic drum manufacturer offers a kit that is bundled with every component, module, and pad that you need to get started. Many companies also offer an electronic kit at each price point, ranging from beginner (inexpensive) to professional (very expensive). Thus, like most products on the market, this allows the consumer to choose a product based upon their individual budget, desire, and overall skill level. Let's take a look at an average electronic drum kit and its components:

THE MODULE

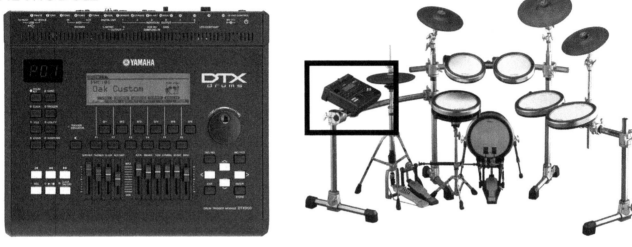

Fig. 1.2

A drum module is an electronic musical instrument that is similar to a synthesizer. Instead of generating sounds, it models sounds or uses recordings, i.e. samples, of sounds that are recorded into it by the manufacturer (and oftentimes by the user). Within the context of a full electronic kit, it also acts as "command central" because it interprets the incoming signals from each pad, processes the signal, and then plays a corresponding sound that is stored within in its memory. For example:

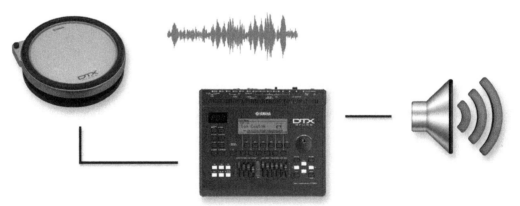

Fig. 1.3. The Function of a Drum Module

In addition, most modules function, operate, and navigate in a similar fashion. They each use function buttons, located on the face, that correspond to different aspects of operation. Let's take a look at the front panel of a typical electronic drum module:

Screen: In the center of the face, there is an LED display that indicates the kit name, song name, or any other user selectable parameter (or important information). Submenus are also usually visible within these windows.

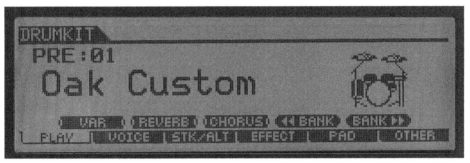

Fig. 1.4

Drum Kit Selector: This allows you to select the kit that you would like to play. The selector is usually controlled by a mod wheel (or arrows) that is used to scroll through different kit selections.

Song Selector: This allows you to select the song you wish to play. Again, you would use a mod wheel (or arrows) to scroll through the different song selections.

Mixer: The mixer allows you to balance the volume of each kit component with moving (slide-able) faders. Therefore, you can customize your kit levels between the kick drum, snare, toms, and cymbals. If you are playing to a song on an MP3 player or the on-board accompaniment, there is usually a fader for that too. Finally, you can also set all of the individual component volumes to one desired level with the master volume fader.

Let's take a look at all three:

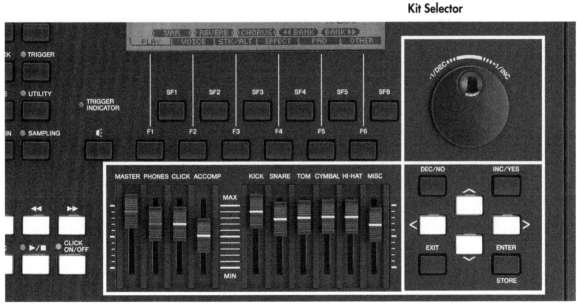

Fig. 1.5

DRUM TRIGGER PADS

Trigger pads are synthetic drum playing surfaces, very reminiscent to a traditional practice pad in both appearance and feel. In a standard kit configuration, each pad corresponds to a traditional acoustic drum voice: the bass drum, snare drum, toms, hi-hat, and cymbals. Each pad is also connected to the electronic drum module by ¼" cable, which when struck, sends a signal to the module to produce the appropriate drum sound (see Fig. 1.3 on page 12).

Playing Surfaces

Trigger pads come in all shapes, sizes, and materials. The three most common materials used are rubber, mesh, and silicone. Historically, rubber is the most widely produced because it is inexpensive to manufacture. This is why it is used on thousands of practice pads!

In the mid-1990s, Roland introduced the first mesh headed drum pad. This type of pad feels quite uniform on all surfaces (snare, toms, bass drum), and it offers a much better rebound than traditional rubber. In 2010, DTX Drums by Yamaha introduced a textured cellular silicone pad. This DTX pad allows for feel and tension variations, i.e., the snare drum pad has a tighter rebound and more response than a floor tom pad.

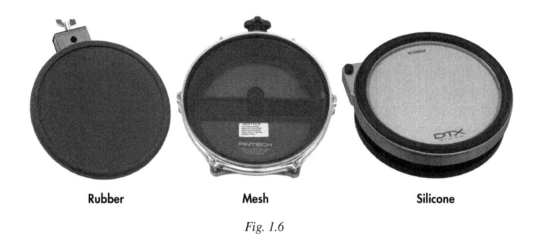

| Rubber | Mesh | Silicone |

Fig. 1.6

Zones

A zone is a sub-pad within the playing surface where you assign a sound. No matter what playing material you choose, all trigger pads offer either a single, double, or triple zone surface. Let's take a look at all three types of zones.

A single zone pad has one area to assign a sound:

Snare Sound

Fig. 1.7

A double zone pad has two areas to assign a sound:

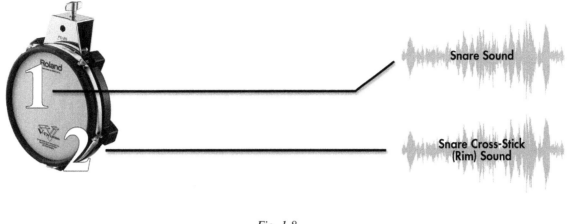

Fig. 1.8

A triple zone pad has three areas to assign a sound:

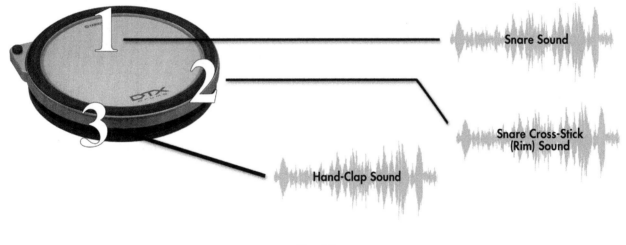

Fig. 1.9

Take a look at figure 1.9. This triple zone pad could have three available sounds assigned to it: the center zone could have a snare, the second zone a snare cross stick (rim), and the third zone a hand clap. On some more advanced modules, you can even layer multiple sounds onto one zone. Again, you could potentially play all three sounds—the snare, cross stick, and hand clap—with one stroke on the center of the pad.

CYMBAL TRIGGER PADS

Cymbal trigger pads function just like drum trigger pads. They are round or triangular in shape and made of rubber. They can also have one, two, or three zones.

**Single Zone Cymbal Pad
(One Sound)**

**Double Zone Cymbal Pad
(Two Sounds)**

**Triple Zone Cymbal Pad
(Three Sounds)**

Fig. 1.10

In Fig. 1.10, you can clearly see all three types of cymbal pads. Using the triple zone pad as an example, you can use a ride cymbal sound on zone 1, a bell sound on zone 2, and a crash (edge) sound on zone 3. For example:

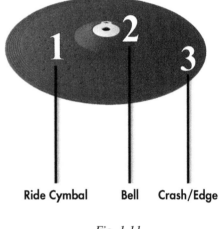

Ride Cymbal   Bell   Crash/Edge

Fig. 1.11

HARDWARE: STANDS AND RACKS

Electronic drum kit manufacturers place their drum and cymbal pads on racks. They do this for several reasons:

- the kit is completely self-contained and modular.

- it's easy to set up, use, and store.

- it would be quite cumbersome to put each lightweight drum and cymbal pad on its own freestanding snare, tom, or cymbal stand.

This being said (and for an acoustic drummer's comfort), the snare and hi-hat trigger pads are usually placed on a lightweight stand within the rack setup. Here are two examples of high end rack setups (on the following page):

Yamaha   **Roland**

Fig. 1.12

On less expensive lightweight kits, the snare is oftentimes placed on the rack like this:

Yamaha   **Roland**

Fig. 1.13

CABLES

Cables are very important to (and necessary for) electronic drumming. Instrument cables connect the output of each trigger pad (and send signals) directly into the electronic drum module. There are two types of ¼" instrument cables and each has a different connector type. They are: ¼" TS connectors and ¼" TRS connectors.

TS Cable Connector

A TS cable is the most common connector. TS is an abbreviation for tip and sleeve. The hot wire of the cable connects to the tip; the ground (usually the shielding) attaches to the sleeve. This connector can carry one signal from a single zone pad to the module.

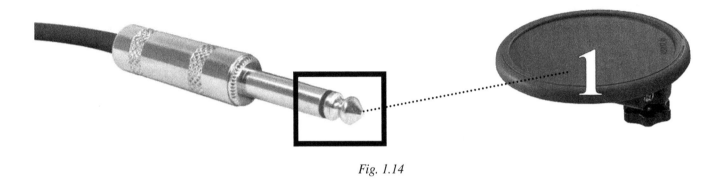

Fig. 1.14

This connector can also carry two signals from a double zone pad to the module:

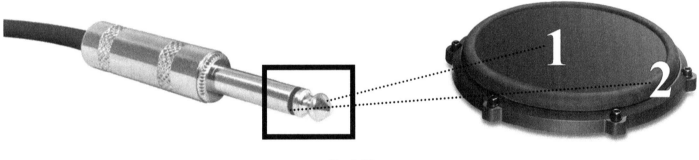

Fig. 1.15

TRS Cable Connector

This jack looks like the TS ¼" connector but has an extra segment in the shaft called the ring. The tip, ring, and sleeve allow the connection of two wires as well as a ground. This connector carries two signals from a double zone pad—or three signals from a triple zone pad—to the module.

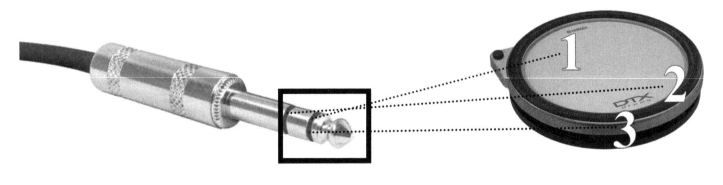

Fig. 1.16

CONNECTING THE COMPONENTS

THE MODULE IS CLEARLY LABELED

Each manufacturer makes hooking up the components to the module a straightforward endeavor. Each input and output on the module is clearly labeled. Therefore, you will see each pad's input labeled as kick, hi-hat, crash2, crash1, ride, toms1–4, and snare. Each output is also labeled: individual output 1–6, stereo output L/R, and phones. For example:

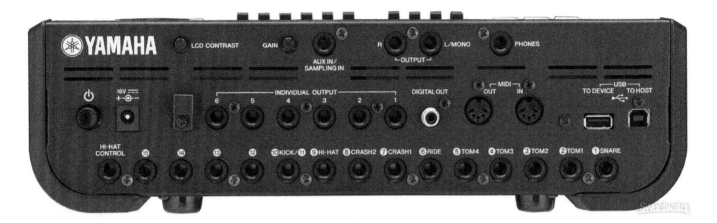

Fig. 1.17

CONNECT THE DRUM PADS TO THE MODULE

To accomplish this, you connect a cable between the pad's output and its corresponding input on the module. Therefore, to use the kick as an example, the output of the kick pad would connect by ¼" TS cable to the input on the module like this:

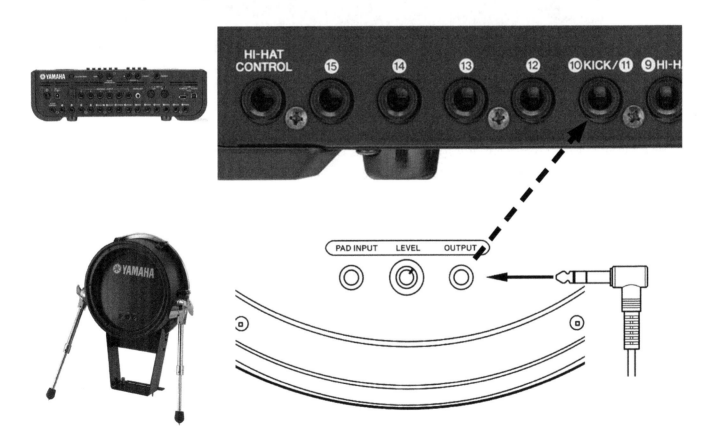

Fig. 1.18

CONNECT THE CYMBAL PADS TO THE MODULE

The cymbal pads connect to the module in the same fashion as the drum pads. However, many cymbal pads have two cables. For example, the hi-hat has different sounds depending on whether it is open, closed, or somewhere in between. Therefore, this trigger pad has two outputs and cables attached to it. They are usually labeled hi-hat and hi-hat control. You simply connect both of these pad outputs to the designated inputs on the module. For example:

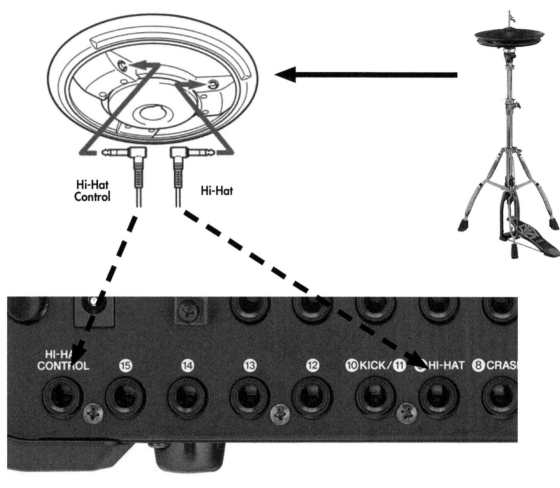

Fig. 1.19

STEREO OUTPUTS: THE MODULE TO A PA AND HEADPHONES

There are three main outputs on most drum modules: a stereo output that consists of a left/mono and right channel (outputs 1 and 2), and a headphone output (output 3). In order to hear your drum kit, you should connect one or both of the following:

- The stereo outputs (left and right) to an amplifier (speaker set)

- Your headphones to the phones output on the module

Now you are ready to play!

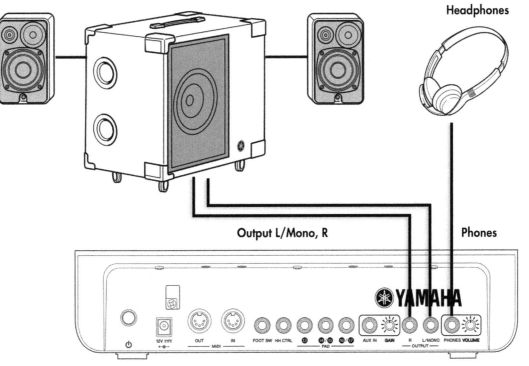

Fig. 1.20

INDIVIDUAL OUTS: DETAILED MIXING AND MONITORING

In addition to the stereo outputs, many of today's modules have multiple (individual) outputs. These can be assigned to individual drum pads (drum sounds) for an extremely detailed mix. For example, let's say you would like to send your entire kit to the house PA, but you would like the snare drum to have compression, EQ, and reverb applied by the sound man. You could send the entire kit to the stereo outputs, and the snare drum to individual output 1. Most modules also feature auxiliary (AUX) inputs and digital outputs. Oftentimes, the auxiliary input is used to send an iPod into the module (for play-along purposes), and the digital output can be connected to a recording interface for an additional recording signal. Here is one common multi-output scenario:

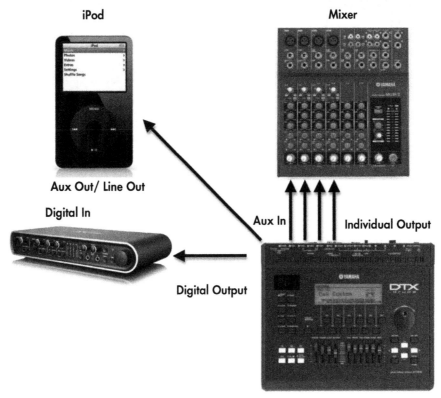

Fig. 1.21

Note: You can still send the stereo outputs to an amplifier and plug in your headphones as in Fig. 1.20.

THE RACK

Drummers come in all shapes and sizes. Therefore, one size does not fit all when it comes to racks and stands. Most drummers set their kits up to suit their height and overall body type. The racks and stands have positional settings so that you can raise or lower and adjust the angles of the different components. There are no rules, but I strongly urge new drummers to seek proper instruction regarding the ergonomics of drumming. You can develop some bad habits that can lead to aches and pains if you do not pay attention to your posture when you play.

CABLE MANAGEMENT

Keep it clean and tidy! Most manufacturers include cable clips or Velcro® ties that you can use to attach the cables to the rack. Some manufacturers even include materials for making a snake. A snake is a bunch of cables banded together to make one big cable. The more you organize (and take care of) your cables, the longer they will last and function properly.

Cable Clips   **Velcro Ties**   **Cable Snake**

Fig. 1.22

Fig. 1.23. Velcro Ties Used on a Drum Rack

ADDITIONAL ITEMS

Now that we have discussed the full electronic drum kit, let's take a look at some additional (and helpful) items that you may need. These do not come packaged with your electronic drum kit.

MONITORS

Most electronic drum manufacturers offer monitoring systems that are made for, and are compatible with, their electronic drum kits. They usually offer a good, better, and best type of selection. These monitoring systems are used for personal monitoring during practice; they are not usually intended for a live performance. Here are some things to keep in mind when choosing a monitor system:

- The better the system, the better the quality of your drum sound. If you are buying a lower priced, or introductory, electronic drum kit, most of the available monitor systems will do the job. However, when your kit has a higher sound quality than your monitoring system, you may miss the low frequency projection within your kick drum and low tom samples.

- For the highest quality reproduction of sound, your monitor system needs to have a woofer for low frequencies and dual tweeters for high frequencies. These two speaker types are usually separated. The woofer is placed on the floor and the tweeters are elevated as satellite speakers like this:

Fig. 1.24

Here are two of the most popular style monitor systems for electronic drums:

Fig. 1.25

HEADPHONES

If your mom, dad, sister, brother, girlfriend, boyfriend, or significant other does not want to hear you practice, you will need a set of headphones. As with all items, price dictates the quality of the phones. Therefore, you should study and compare the frequency capabilities from headphone to headphone. The wider the frequency range, the better the headphones will reproduce each sound of the drum kit. Try as many pairs as you can and let your ears decide which model is for you.

Type

You should look at both "open" and "closed" ear types as well. Choosing a proper set of headphones is based on comfort and frequency response.

Open-Ear Headphones   Closed-Ear Headphones

Fig. 1.26

> **Special note:** Protect your hearing! Do not turn up your monitors or headphones to levels that can damage your hearing. Unlike acoustic drumsets, we can control the volume level of electronic drum kits. Therefore, it is important that you take advantage of the volume control knob. You will be glad you did when you are older.

MIXING BOARD

As previously discussed, most electronic modules come with a small on-board audio mixer that allows you to achieve a nice balance within each drumset voice. This mixer is usually intended for practice or small venue performance situations. You may also encounter other playing situations where you need to send multiple mixes to the house PA, house monitor system, and multiple band members—all at the same time. This is common within many larger live venues, and if this is the case, you will need a mixing board. Just use the on-board individual outputs on the back of your module to send each drumset voice to your stage mixing board. This stage mixer will then redistribute your drum kit sounds. Professional mixing boards vary greatly in both price and features. Therefore—and for more detailed information on mixers—I encourage you to consult a mixing professional.

MP3 PLAYER, iPOD

If you don't have one, get one. You will have a lot of fun playing your electronic drum kit to songs on your MP3 player. As mentioned previously, most of the kits have an auxiliary input on the module, which will allow you to mix your MP3s alongside the electronic drum kit voices.

MY SETUP

Now that we have discussed the full electric drum kit, let's take a look at my setup:

REFERENCE AUDIO

For further understanding of the full electronic kit, please listen to the audio tracks listed below.
I have also notated the three grooves that I performed within the drum kit patches for your study as well.

Maple Drum Kit

In this groove example, I am playing a half-time shuffle.

Techno Drum Kit

In this groove example, I am playing a four-on-the-floor, two-handed sixteenth-note hi-hat pattern.

Motown Drum Kit

In this groove example, I am playing a standard 1960s R&B pattern.

CHAPTER TWO
Percussion Pads

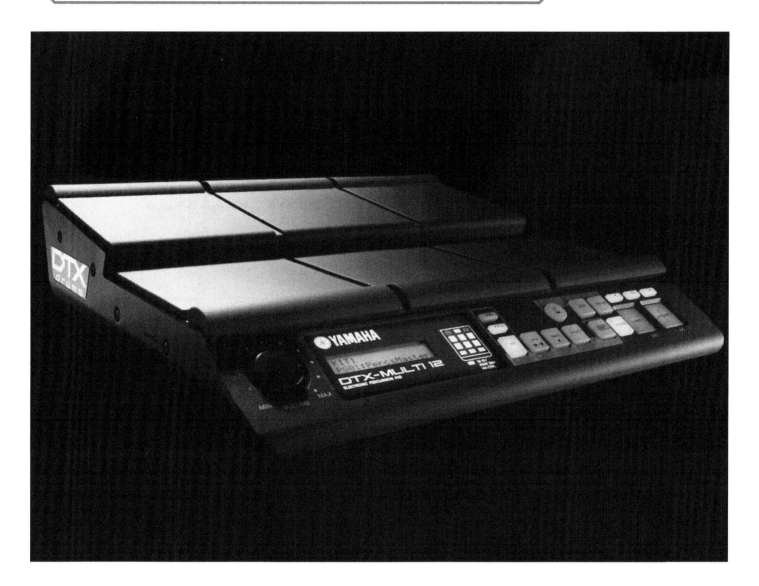

Prominent Electronic Drum Manufacturers	Predominant Models
Yamaha	DTX-MULTI12, DD-65
Roland	SPD-30, SPD-20, SPDS, SPDS-SX
Alesis	Performance & Performance Pad Pro
Simmons	Digital Multi-Pad, SDMK4, SD1 Practice Pad

Electronic percussion pads act much like a full electronic drum kit. However, each of your sounds and trigger pads are self-contained in one freestanding unit. This pad can augment your traditional acoustic or full electronic drum kit, and it *usually* contains eight (or more) on-board pads that can trigger any conceivable electronic voice. These can range from the normal bass drum, snare drum, toms, hi-hat, and cymbals samples to various ethnic shakers, tambourines, congas, and keyboard instruments. Just as with the drum module from chapter 1, this "all-in-one" pad has rear trigger inputs that you can use to connect to various sources such as signal triggers, foot trigger pedals, or even traditional electronic (full-size) triggers pads. Thus, this unit can also act as the central nervous system of your setup.

In this chapter, I will present the advantages of using (and the many professional uses for) the percussion pad. In addition, a detailed description of each component, how to hook each up, audio samples, and a quick look at my percussion pad setup will also be discussed. Please note that each detailed example focuses on units that are completely self-contained, i.e., all of the pads and sounds are on-board in one single unit. Here are some of the most widely used percussion pads:

Yamaha DTX

Roland

Simmons

Alesis

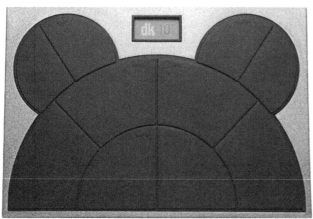

Alternate Mode drumKat

Roland

Fig. 2.1

PERCUSSION PAD ADVANTAGES

There are many advantages to using a percussion pad. Most importantly, you have a complete array of sounds within one small transportable unit, which also includes both the on-board module and trigger pads. In addition (and depending on how robust your electronic pad is), these pads can contain everything from acoustic drums sounds to percussion sounds to tuned percussion instruments. Additionally, your pad will probably come preloaded with loops and drum grooves for you to practice with. Oftentimes, the robust models also allow you to record your own samples and loops into the unit.

There are three basic uses for this type of instrument:

1. It can be used as a stand-alone percussion tool.

2. It can be used to augment your acoustic drum kit.

3. It can be used as a music production tool.

Let's take a look at each in greater detail:

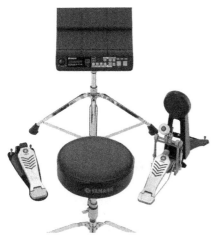

Fig. 2.2

STAND-ALONE

As previously stated, you can have many different percussion instruments in one small (and ultra-portable) package. Using a pair of sticks, your hands, or even your fingers, you can easily play without any additional equipment. Essentially, this pad can be used as a portable, compact, and oftentimes less expensive alternative to a full electronic drum kit. Thus, in an instant you can dial up a full kit with kick, snare, tom, and cymbal sounds, as well as numerous percussion sounds such as wood blocks, bongos, congas, triangles, and tuned percussion (vibraphone, marimba, and timpani). If you add a bass drum and hi-hat trigger pedal, this pad is now a "kit."

Fig. 2.3

ADD TO YOUR ACOUSTIC KIT

Using a percussion pad alongside your acoustic drum kit is probably the most common advantage (and use for) this type of device. Whether you're playing in a Top 40 band, doing pickup gigs, or working in an original project, this pad can enhance your acoustic drum performance. You will be able to seamlessly add triggered hand claps, tambourine, wood block, or auxiliary snare drums to your songs. As you become more advanced, you can also play to on-board loops and patterns, or program loops into it and accompany them by playing your acoustic drums. This device can also replace your metronome by using the on-board click for tempo settings, both during practice sessions and gigs.

Fig. 2.4

MUSIC PRODUCTION

Drummers, DJs, and music producers can also use percussion pads in the recording studio. These pads are more fun to play than a MIDI keyboard, which makes them the perfect studio component and rhythm production tool. By using a percussion pad alongside studio production software such as Cubase, Nuendo, Logic, Ableton Live, or Pro Tools, you can record percussion parts, drum grooves, or keyboard instruments into your compositions. As most pads are very tactile, performances can be accomplished with sticks, hands, or fingers.

COMPONENTS

Unlike the components that make up a full electronic drum kit in chapter 1, the percussion pad is much more straightforward. The module and the trigger pads are self-contained in one unit, which eliminates the need for any connect cables from your triggers to your module. Therefore, striking an individual pad triggers an on-board sample and produces a sound.

Again, most electronic drum manufacturers offer a percussion pad at each price point, ranging from beginner (inexpensive) to professional (very expensive). Thus, like most products on the market, this allows the consumer to choose a product based upon their individual budget, desire, and overall skill level. The percussion pad has many of the same attributes as the module on a full electronic drum kit. Let's take a look at an average percussion pad and its internal and external components:

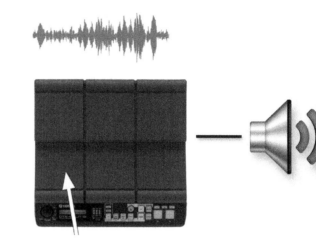

Fig. 2.5

THE MODULE

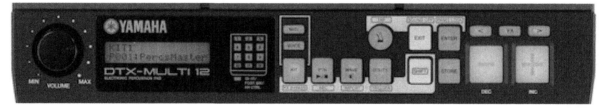

Fig. 2.6

There are preloaded sounds from the manufacturer called presets. You can modify these presets and save them as a custom user kit, and even create additional user kits from scratch. The number of on-board preset sounds—and the capacity to store user sounds—will vary from unit to unit. Many pads also allow you to store and load your own custom sounds on a USB memory device or compact flash card.

A percussion pad module functions, operates, and navigates in a similar fashion to the full drum kit module as well. It utilizes function buttons, located on the face, that correspond to different operations. Let's take a look at the front panel of a typical electronic drum percussion pad.

Screen: On the face, there is an LCD display that indicates important selectable information and user data. Submenus are also usually visible within these windows.

Fig. 2.7

Volume Control Knob: This dial controls the master volume, i.e., the volume at the output jacks. You can turn the dial clockwise to increase the volume or counterclockwise to decrease it.

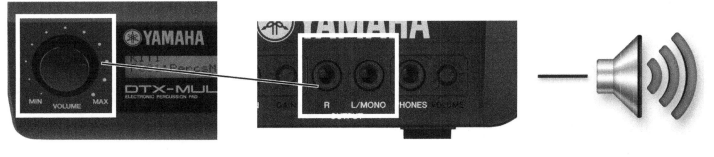

Fig. 2.8

Pad Indicator: As you strike the various pads, this array of LEDs shows which pads have been struck and that they are producing sound. This is helpful during detailed editing and assigning sounds to each pad.

Fig. 2.9

Voice: This button allows you to select and edit the voices (preset voices, wave files, and patterns) assigned to each of the individual pads.

Kit: This button allows you to access the on-board kit presets, or the custom user kits, that you have created and stored.

Pattern, WAVE, Utility, Shift: These buttons are used to access various areas that enable you to record patterns, import files, and perform a range of file management operations.

Enter, Exit, Store: These buttons allow you to execute processes and store them within the memory of the unit.

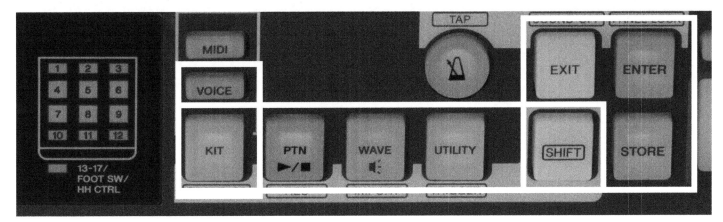

Fig. 2.10

TAP: Tap is commonly used as part of a metronome function. Some units allow a user to "tap" several notes in succession. Afterward, the module will determine and display the BPM (beats per minute) of the combined strokes.

Arrows: These buttons allow you to navigate horizontally and vertically. This helps to select various parameters in the settings area of the module.

Dec and Inc (+/-): When navigating with the arrows, these buttons allow you to increase or decrease values.

Fig. 2.11

TRIGGER PADS

As I mentioned, a percussion pad has a number of trigger pads condensed into one unit. There is one drawback: these pads are much smaller than what you see on a full electronic drum kit. You must be more accurate with your stroke, especially if you are playing with sticks within a dimly lit environment. Additionally, these trigger pads are limited to one zone, but on some models you can stack (layer) multiple sounds on a single zone. You can get four to twelve pads within the same amount of space as one regular-sized, three-zone trigger pad. Below are shown three popular pad models. They have eight, ten, and twelve pads respectively.

Fig. 2.12

PLAYING SURFACE

Unlike some of the newer materials that we have seen in drum and cymbal triggers, the surface of a percussion pad is made of either soft rubber or hard rubber. This can make the surface more challenging to play when using a stick.

Soft Rubber   **Hard Rubber**

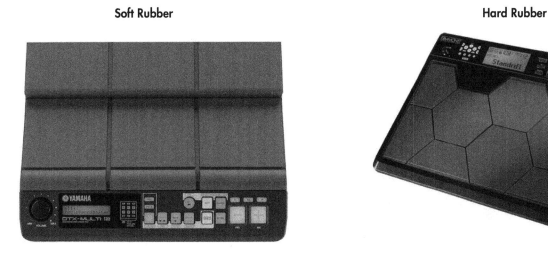

Fig. 2.13

Although the two surfaces above look quite similar, they feel quite different. You should definitely play both before deciding on a model of percussion pad.

STANDS

Electronic drum manufacturers generally sell a stand and a clamp that is used for electronic percussion pads. The clamp mounts to the backside of the percussion pad, and this fitting connects to the stand, which then holds the pad. These are usually not universal; each manufacturer has their own system of clamps and fittings. This also holds true for racks.

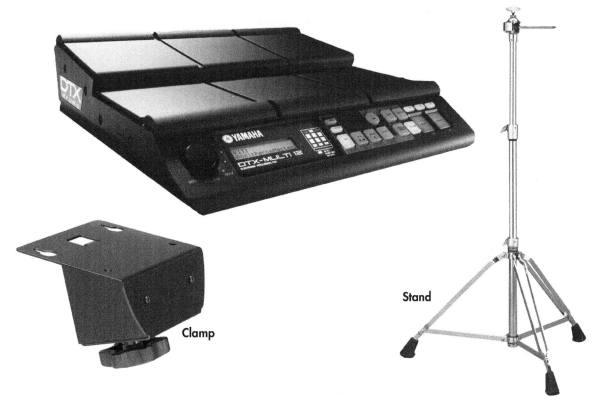

Clamp

Stand

Fig. 2.14

CONNECTIONS

STEREO AND HEADPHONE OUTPUTS

There are three main outputs on most electronic percussion pads: 1. a stereo output that consists of a left/mono 2. a right channel 3. a headphone output

Fig. 2.15

AUXILIARY INPUTS

Most percussion pads also feature auxiliary (AUX) inputs and digital outputs. Oftentimes, the auxiliary input is used to send an iPod into the module (for play along purposes), and the digital output can be connected to a recording interface for an additional recording input.

Fig. 2.16

In order to hear your percussion pad, you should connect one (or all) of the following:

- The output jacks (left/mono and right) to an amplifier or set of speakers

- Your headphones to the phones jack

- Your MP3 player to the AUX IN

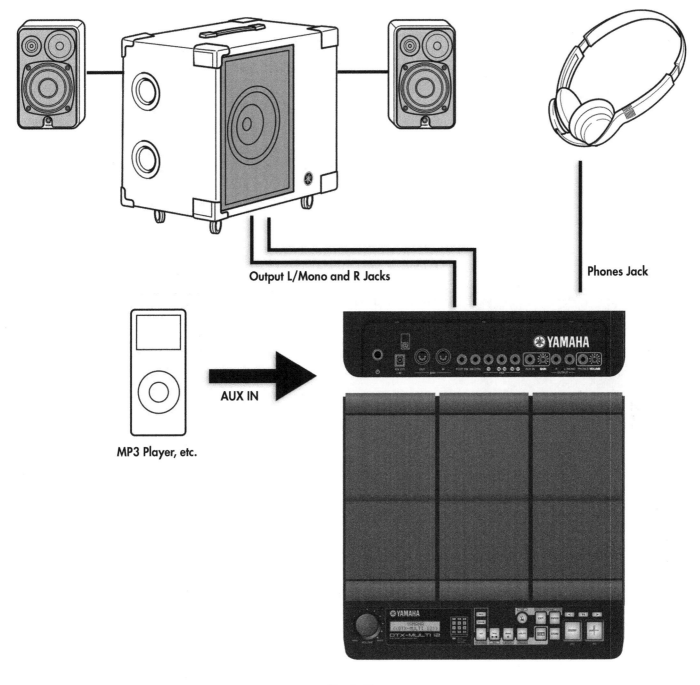

Fig. 2.17

SPECIALIZED PERCUSSION PADS 1

HAND, MALLET, AND UNIQUE PADS

There are some electronic drum pads on the market that are considered percussion pads, but they have characteristics that are a bit different from the standard type. These pads can have one surface, or many, and they are sensitive to pressure, texture (scratching), and positioning. These attributes make them perfect for percussionists that use their hands and a wide variety of mallets.

Fig. 2.18

Korg Wavedrum

This instrument is one single pad surface that can be played with sticks, mallets, or hands. It's classified as a synthesizer, and it is responsive to pressure by rubbing or scratching. It can be used to play melodic or percussive phrases too. It has many cultural and ethnic percussion sounds and traditional drum kit sounds on board.

Fig. 2.19

Roland Handsonic

The Roland Handsonic is an electronic hand percussion pad with fifteen trigger pads. Each pad's built-in pressure sensor allows for realistic muting, and depending on the area of the pad that is hit, the timbre of the sound will change.

Fig. 2.20

Mandala Pad

The Mandala electronic pad is a single surface device that connects to a computer via USB. It has eighteen zones, which all respond to pressure, pitch bend, and location-based strikes. Thus, it responds much like an acoustic drum. It can also be used to modify the sounds of keyboard and other pitched instruments. This pad and software package comes with 4GB of modifiable sounds.

SPECIALIZED PERCUSSION PADS 2: MIDI CONTROLLERS

TRADITIONAL MIDI CONTROLLERS

MIDI allows performers to control multiple synthesizers from a single keyboard. Most controllers do not have any internal sounds, but these devices transmit MIDI data to external sound modules (synthesizers) or computer software synthesizers that produce sound. For example:

MIDI Channel 1 (Send)
MIDI Keyboard Controller
without Internal Sound

Hardware Drum Machine

Software Sampler

Fig. 2.21

PERCUSSION PAD MIDI CONTROLLERS

Pad controllers are the modern percussion equivalent to the traditional MIDI keyboard controller. Usually, this device has four to twelve on-board trigger pads that are used to trigger external sound sources. These include a laptop running various software synthesizers, sequencers, or hardware drum machines. Oftentimes, performers choose a pad controller because they can constantly update and augment their sounds with external laptops, modules, and sample libraries. This helps to keep their sounds current without upgrading their percussion pad hardware every few years.

MIDI Percussion Pad Controller without Internal Sounds

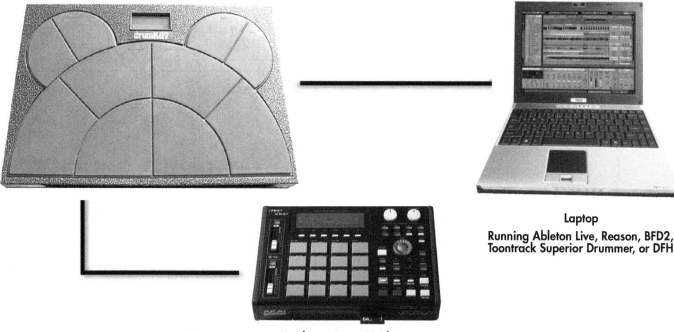

Laptop
Running Ableton Live, Reason, BFD2, Toontrack Superior Drummer, or DFH

Hardware Drum Machine

Fig. 2.22

The drumKAT

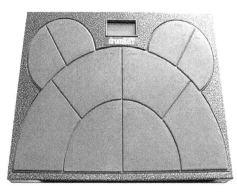

Fig. 2.23

The Alternate Mode drumKAT was the first well-known and widely used pad controller. It has ten pads and nine rear trigger inputs for additional pedals and remote trigger pads. Again, it has no sounds of its own, but its real strength is its on-board software that allows you to stack multiple notes on the same pad (in some cases, up to 128 different sounds per pad). In addition, each pad can alternate through 8–128 sounds per pad (depending on the model), and there are four sets of MIDI inputs and outputs. Thus, you can connect to sixty-four separate devices (sound sources) via the MIDI protocol.

The trapKAT

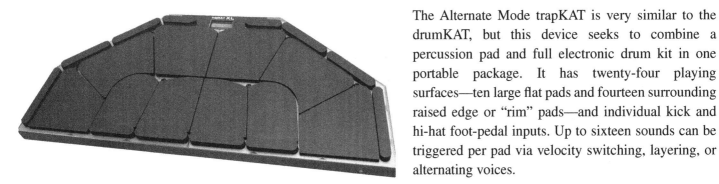

Fig. 2.24

The Alternate Mode trapKAT is very similar to the drumKAT, but this device seeks to combine a percussion pad and full electronic drum kit in one portable package. It has twenty-four playing surfaces—ten large flat pads and fourteen surrounding raised edge or "rim" pads—and individual kick and hi-hat foot-pedal inputs. Up to sixteen sounds can be triggered per pad via velocity switching, layering, or alternating voices.

Additional Controllers

There are hundreds of percussion controllers on the market. The two KAT products are the most common, but there are many more, most of which are played with your fingers instead of sticks and connect to a computer via USB. Here are two of the most popular:

Akai MPD Series   **Korg Nano Series**

Fig. 2.25

ADDITIONAL ITEMS

If you choose to go the MIDI percussion pad controller route, you will need some additional items beyond the full kit items listed in chapter 1, starting on page 23.

MIDI to USB Interface

A MIDI to USB interface will connect from the MIDI inputs and outputs of your percussion pad controller to a laptop or desktop computer. Here is an example of a simple MIDI interface:

Entire Cable   **Cable Close Up**   **Connection Overview**

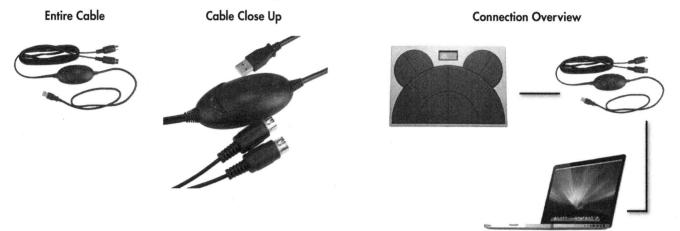

Fig. 2.26

Connection Close Up

Connect the MIDI In and MIDI Out of the USB MIDI Interface to the MIDI Out and MIDI In of the pad controller:

Fig. 2.27

Then, connect the USB portion of the M-Audio Interface into the USB port on the laptop:

Fig. 2.28

DETAILED CONNECTION EXAMPLE

Using the additional items from chapters 1 and 2, one popular example of a percussion pad controller setup and connection schematic is shown below.

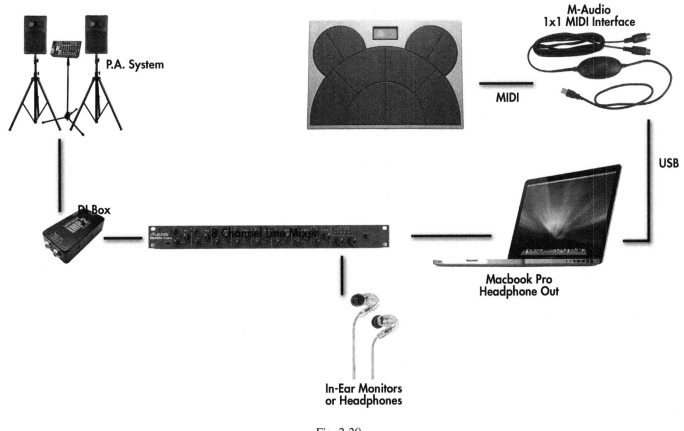

Fig. 2.29

MIDI AND SOFTWARE DISCLAIMER

This book is the *beginners* guide to electronic drums. Therefore, if you would like to familiarize yourself with detailed MIDI concepts or the available software packages on the market, I suggest that you consult additional texts on these subjects. Some of the most popular software packages for drum triggering are listed below:

Software	Web Site
Reason	www.propellerheads.se
Ableton Live	www.ableton.com
BFD2	www.fxpansion.com
Superior Drummer	www.toontrack.com

MY SETUP

Now that we have discussed the percussion pad, let's take a look at my setup:

REFERENCE AUDIO

For further understanding of the percussion pad, please listen to the audio tracks listed below. I have also notated the groove that I performed within the drum kit patch as well.

Drum Kit Groove

In this example, I played the following groove:

CHAPTER THREE
Signal Triggers –
Building a Hybrid Kit

Electronic Drum Trigger Manufacturers	
Ddrum	Roland
Pintech	Pulse
Yamaha	Aquarian
Simmons	

In this chapter, I will present the advantages of using (and the many professional uses for) signal triggers alongside a hybrid acoustic-electronic drum kit. A detailed description of how to hook up signal triggers with our previously mentioned components and audio samples, and a quick look at my setup, will also be presented.

Ddrum Pro

Ddrum Red Shot

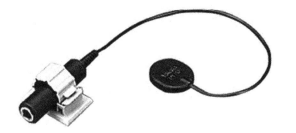

Roland

Pintech

Yamaha

Pulse

Simmons

Pintech Trigger Perfect

Fig. 3.1

HYBRID ADVANTAGES: ADDING SIGNAL TRIGGERS

A hybrid drum kit allows you to combine acoustic and electronic percussion into one setup. Whether you're a pro drummer playing with the top artists in the world, or a Top 40 band in a small club, you can alternate between your acoustic drums and electronic full kit, or combine them together into your performances.

With these facts in mind, let's assume that you're at a gig. The first tune of the night only needs acoustic drums; but then the next two songs are both up-tempo dance tunes. These require a synthetic sounding snare drum and "boomy" electro-bass drum. In a hybrid scenario, you could place signal triggers on your acoustic snare and bass drum. As you play, both triggers would send signals to your drum module and trigger the appropriate sounds alongside your acoustic kit. For example:

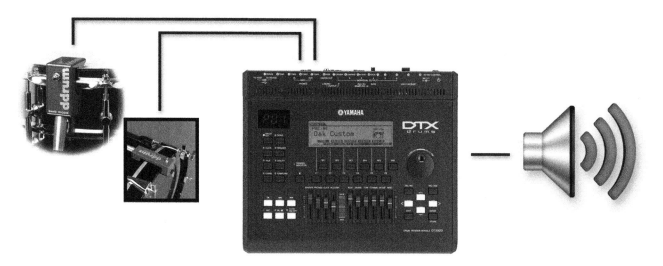

Fig. 3.2

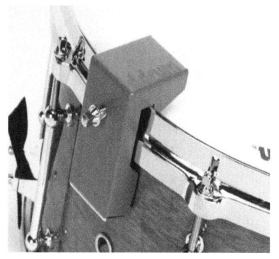

Fig. 3.3

ADDING SIGNAL TRIGGERS

In the last two chapters, we discussed drum, cymbal, and self-contained percussion pad triggers. However, there is another form of trigger called a "signal trigger." It clamps onto an acoustic drum, and its sensor detects the stick strikes that occur on the drumhead. The signal trigger converts this strike into an electrical impulse, and sends it via a cable to the module, percussion pad, or controller, which produces a sound (see Fig. 3.1 above). There are several different types of signal triggers. They can come in many shapes, sizes, materials, and manners in which they attach to the acoustic drumhead. You can buy signal triggers individually, and many companies make pre-configured packs that include a bass drum, snare, and three-tom triggers.

Adhesive Style Triggers

The most common trigger is made of plastic with an adhesive that you press onto the drumhead. Oftentimes with this type of trigger, a two-sided tape is needed, as the adhesive tends to break down over time. This type comes in two sizes: a typical snare drum trigger is the size of a nickel, and a kick drum trigger is a bit larger.

| Adhesive Signal Trigger | Adhesive Snare Trigger | Adhesive Bass Drum Trigger |

Fig. 3.4

Clamp Style Triggers

Other signal triggers are more sophisticated. Oftentimes, these are made of metal, and they clamp onto the rim of the drum. These tend to work better and last longer, as they are much sturdier in design. (After all, they are intended to withstand the effects of a drum being hit with a stick.) You can also change drumheads without damaging the transducer, and the metal casing protects the trigger from accidental drum hits. These triggers do not muffle the drumhead.

Ddrum Clamp Style Triggers

Roland Clamp Style Triggers

Fig. 3.5

No matter what type of signal trigger you use, each type will either be connected to a drum module or percussion pad via cable. For example:

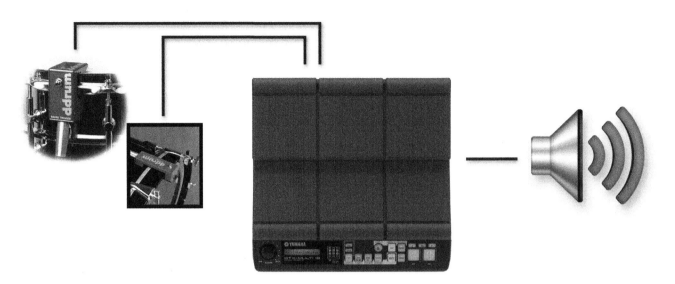

Fig. 3.6

Single and Double Zone

Just as with electronic pads, signal triggers can have multiple zones, i.e., sensors. Usually, bass drums and toms utilize a single sensor trigger. The snare drum usually features a double zone trigger: the first zone picks up the snare head signals, and the second transducer—also mounted in the housing—senses rim shots, cross stick, or anything played on the drum's hoop. For example:

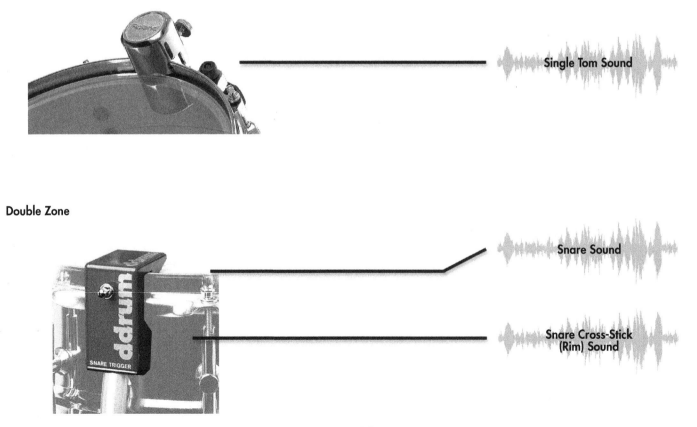

Fig. 3.7

Placement of Signal Triggers

Signal triggers are usually placed one inch away from the rim. Remember, the only thing a signal trigger is doing is getting a sympathetic vibration, or signal. It does not act as a microphone or pick up sound. When placing your triggers, you should: (1) place them in areas where you will not strike them with your sticks (2) put them in areas where the cables can run to your module without getting in the way of your hands, feet, or moving parts such as the hi-hat and kick drum pedal.

Adhesive Style Placement

In the example below, you will notice that the bass drum trigger is high enough to avoid being hit by the bass drum beater, and the snare trigger is also out of the way of a traditional rim shot and cross-stick stick placement.

Fig. 3.8

Clamp Style Placement

In a clamp style scenario, the placement (one inch inward) has been taken care of for you. Therefore, I suggest that you place one on the bass drum at the upper-top or side of the batter head. The placement for the snare and toms should be near (or at) the top of the drumhead too.

Bass Drum
(Batter head top or side)   **Tom**
(Batter head top or side)   **Snare**
(Top)

Fig. 3.9

CABLES

Signal triggers connect to a module with a cable. The adhesive style triggers have a ¼" female output that connects to a module with a ¼" male instrument cable like this:

Adhesive Trigger (Female Output)   **¼" Male Instrument Cable**

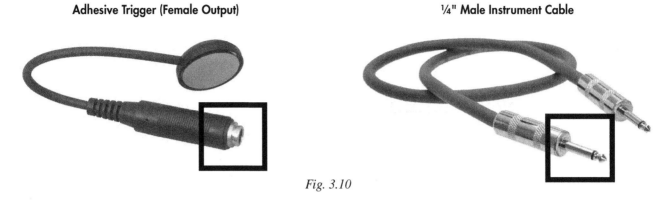

Fig. 3.10

Many of the clamp style triggers use a male XLR output that connects to a module with female XLR to ¼" mono cable like this:

Clamp Style Trigger (Male XLR Output)   **Female XLR to ¼" Mono Cable**

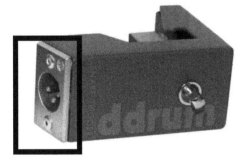
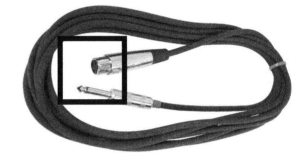

Fig. 3.11

Double Zone Cable

However, if you are also using a dual (two) zone trigger, you will need a cable that transmits two signals. One example is a female XLR to two ¼" male Y cables like this:

Double Zone Snare Trigger   **Female XLR to Two ¼" Male Y Cables**

Fig. 3.12

HYBRID SETUP 1: CONNECTING THE COMPONENTS

ACOUSTIC KIT WITH MODULE AND SIGNAL TRIGGERS

If you already have (or plan on purchasing) a full electronic kit, this first setup may be perfect for you. If you have already read chapter 1, just replace the drum and cymbal pads with acoustic signal triggers. Then, as you strike your acoustic kit, you will be playing both the electronic and natural acoustic sounds simultaneously for a true electro-acoustic hybrid setup.

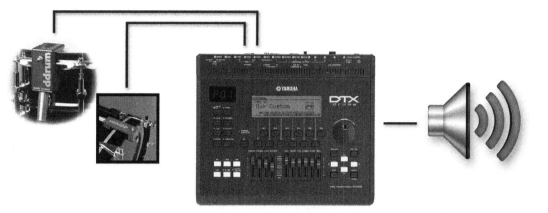

Fig. 3.13

CONNECTING THE TRIGGERS TO YOUR MODULE

Each manufacturer makes hooking up the components to the module a straightforward endeavor. Each input and output on the module is clearly labeled. Therefore, you will see each pad input labeled as kick, snare, and toms 1–4. Just connect the corresponding signal trigger to the proper input on the module as follows:

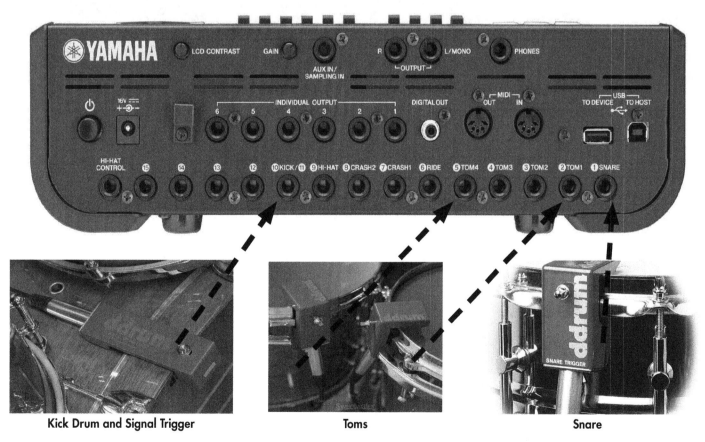

| Kick Drum and Signal Trigger | Toms | Snare |

Fig. 3.14

Note: You can also hook up a combination of electronic pads and signal triggers.

HYBRID SETUP 1: EXAMPLE

Here is a hybrid drum kit example that uses signal triggers and a drum module:

Fig. 3.15

HYBRID SETUP 2: CONNECTING THE COMPONENTS

PERCUSSION PAD WITH MODULE AND SIGNAL TRIGGERS

If you already have (or plan on purchasing) a percussion pad (or controller), this second setup may be perfect for you. If you have already read chapter 2, you are familiar with percussion pads as stand-alone units. However, most of these pads also have additional sets of trigger inputs on the rear of the unit. Just as in the hybrid setup 1, you can connect signal triggers to these inputs and trigger from your acoustic drums. For example:

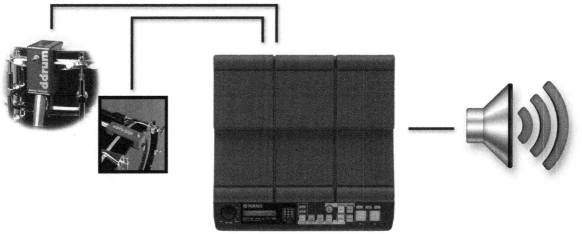

Fig. 3.16

CONNECTING THE TRIGGERS TO YOUR MODULE

Again, each manufacturer makes hooking up the components to the percussion pad a straightforward endeavor. Each input and output on the rear of the unit is clearly labeled. Therefore, you will see each pad input labeled 1–4. Just connect a signal trigger to an input (1–4) on the rear as follows:

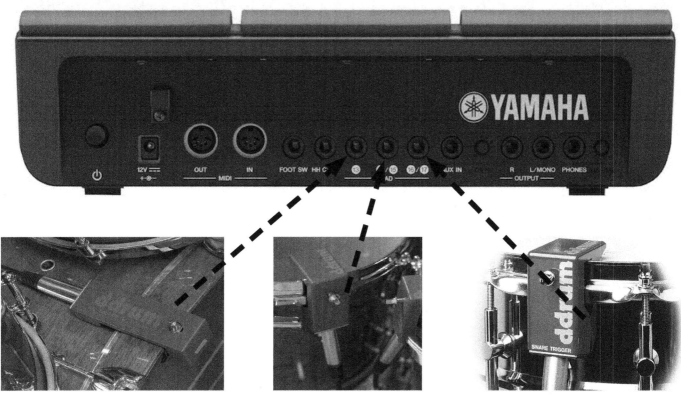

Fig. 3.17

Note: You can also hook up a combination of electronic pads and signal triggers.

SPECIALTY HYBRIDS

HYBRID ACOUSTIC DRUM KIT

Currently, there is one full hybrid kit manufactured by Ddrum, and it includes an acoustic kit with signal triggers built into the shell. The XLR outputs that connect the trigger to the module are also surface mounted.

Fig. 3.18

HYBRID ACOUSTIC CYMBALS

Zildjian manufactures acoustic cymbals called the Gen16AE system. It is a hybrid acoustic/electric cymbal, combining low-volume acoustic cymbals with a microphone, detailed signal processing, and tone modeling. These are not sample trigger devices. Instead, they are actual cymbals that play like normal cymbals, but at reduced volume levels. In addition, these units use a dual microphone to amplify and model the cymbal's output.

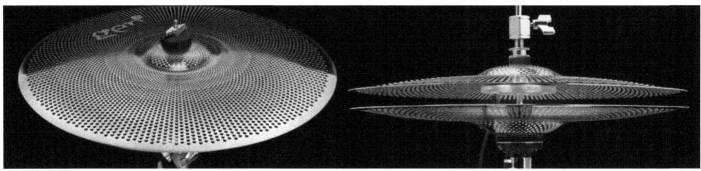

Fig. 3.19

HYBRID ACOUSTIC DRUMHEADS

Aquarian manufactures an acoustic drumhead that has built-in signal triggers. You can hook these into their proprietary inBOX module or any percussion pad/drum module.

Head on a Snare Drum

Internal Trigger

Fig. 3.20

MY SETUP

Now that we have discussed the hybrid drum kit, let's take a look at my setup:

REFERENCE AUDIO

For further understanding of the hybrid drum kit, please listen to the audio tracks listed below. For your study, I have also notated the two grooves that I played as well.

Drum Groove No.1 90 bpm

In this example, I based my groove off the following pattern:

Drum Groove No.2 104 bpm

In this example, I based my groove off the following pattern:

Side by Side Comparisons: